Thomas
GAINSBOROUGH

Artist of England

"Self-Portrait—1754"

Thomas
GAINSBOROUGH

ARTIST OF ENGLAND

by Sally Glendinning

illustrated by Cary

GARRARD PUBLISHING COMPANY
Champaign, Illinois

To my mother, Marie Harrison Wilson,
who made our home at Dreamhaven a place
where fine pictures hung on the walls,
good books lined the shelves,
and music filled the air.

Contents

1. A Day in the Woods

Tom Gainsborough looked out the window of his home on a winding street in Sudbury, England. The sun was shining. The green trees were outlined against the morning sky.

The year was 1737, and Tom Gainsborough was ten years old. He knew he should start for school. The kind headmaster was his uncle. All the children in the school were his friends. If it were raining, Tom would not have minded spending the day in school.

But Tom hated to waste a sunny day indoors

when he could be out sketching. He did not like to study his books, but he would work all day long at his drawing.

Tom wanted to walk through the woods and fields with his paper and pencils. He wanted to draw the curving lines of the road and to sketch trees and bushes. He wanted to copy even the lines of the clouds in the sky.

The headmaster of the Sudbury Grammar School, the Reverend Humphrey Burroughs, would expect a written excuse if Tom were absent. And already Tom's father had written many such excuses.

John Gainsborough, a merchant, was a kind father to all of his nine children. He was especially kind to Tom, the youngest. He realized that it was natural for a boy to want to roam through the woods on a fine day. However, he did not understand why Tom wanted to sketch rather than hunt or fish.

"A day in the woods will do the boy no harm," the father would say. "Tom can read well, and his handwriting already is as good as my own."

When he grew up, Tom painted this portrait of his father, "John Gainsborough."

"Give Tom a Holiday," John Gainsborough would write. Then he would sign his name.

This morning Tom decided to write his own excuse. He knew it was wrong, but he did not think he would be caught.

"Give Tom a Holiday," the boy wrote. He signed his father's name. The handwriting looked exactly like his father's.

Tom stopped by the Sudbury Grammar School long enough to leave the note on the headmaster's desk. Then he was off to visit the woods and meadows outside the town.

He had forgotten to stuff even a piece of bread in his pocket, but he was too busy to be hungry. He sketched a group of trees against the sky. He drew a dusty road with bushes on either side. He spent a long time copying the pattern of a single leaf.

As he walked along the banks of the Stour River, he saw two cows grazing in a nearby field. The cows stood still as he drew their picture. He wished he could color the picture. Perhaps his father would buy him colored chalks or paints soon.

While Tom spent the day outdoors, the headmaster of the school worried about him. How could the boy ever learn his lessons when he took so many holidays? Yet if Tom's father wrote the excuse, what could the headmaster do?

Headmaster Burroughs decided to pay a visit to the Gainsborough home after school. He would speak to Mrs. Gainsborough, his sister. And he would speak to Tom's father.

Tom came home in the late afternoon. He was not able to slip quietly into the house as he had hoped to do. Waiting for him near the front door were his father, his mother, and his school principal.

"Tom, we know that you can copy the line and shape of anything with your pencil," the headmaster said.

"Yes, sir," Tom answered. His rosy cheeks blushed even redder.

"Did you copy my handwriting for the excuse you took to school today?" his father asked.

"Yes, sir," Tom said. He would have liked to explain, but he could think of nothing more to say.

"To copy the way another person signs his name is forgery, and forgery is a crime," Tom's mother said with tears in her eyes.

Tom hung his head in shame. He promised he would forge no more excuses. He promised to go to school every day.

"How did you learn to copy my signature?" his father asked.

"I practiced many times," Tom said. "I will show you my practice papers."

Tom reached for the warming pan that hung from a hook on the wall. On a cold winter night, the long-handled, covered pan was filled with hot coals to warm the beds. The pan was now filled with scraps of paper on which Tom had written "Give Tom a Holiday" in his father's handwriting.

As the boy walked slowly from the room he heard his father say, "Tom will grow up to be hanged!"

Tom knew that bad men were hanged for their crimes. He did not think he had been bad—at least, not that bad. He would show his father the drawings he had made and try to explain.

Late that evening Tom brought his drawings to his father. John Gainsborough looked at them with surprise. He could see that they were good. He recognized the tall trees and dusty road. He smiled at the pictures of the cows grazing in the field.

"Why, anybody would know these drawings were made in the Sudbury woods and meadows," the father said. "I have seen that road many times, but I never saw it as clearly as I do in this drawing."

Tom was happy again. He had not meant to worry his mother and father or to make them ashamed of him.

Tom was even happier as he heard his father say something in a half-whisper to his mother.

"Perhaps our Tom will be a genius!" John Gainsborough said.

2. The Gainsborough Family

Tom Gainsborough did not really want to be a genius. He was not sure what the word "genius" meant. He wanted to be a painter.

His parents, John and Mary Gainsborough, worried about the boy's future. Tom could draw well enough, but could a painter make a living?

Mrs. Gainsborough understood her youngest son's love of art. She liked to paint pictures of flowers as a hobby in her spare time. Usually she was busy managing the big house in Sudbury which once had been an inn.

This busy inn became the Gainsborough home.

The Gainsboroughs needed a house as big as an inn, for there were so many of them. The daughters were named Mary, Sarah, Elizabeth, and Susannah. Mrs. Gainsborough taught them to cook and sew and to take care of a household so that they would be good wives some day.

Then there were the boys. John, the oldest, was named for his father. John was called "Scheming Jack" because he was always trying to invent some new machine.

16

"I have invented a machine that will fly," Scheming Jack said one day. "My flying machine has wings that will carry me through the air."

Scheming Jack carried his machine to a rooftop while his brothers and sisters watched from the road. Scheming Jack jumped off the roof in his machine. The machine did not fly, and neither did Jack. He fell into the ditch with his machine on top of him.

"It's a wonder he didn't break every bone in his body," his mother said.

Scheming Jack also invented a cradle that rocked itself, a mechanical bird that would sing all the year round, and a wheel that turned in a bucket of water.

The second son, Humphrey Gainsborough, also liked to invent. He invented a sundial that is now in the British Museum. But he spent most of his time at his studies, because he wanted to be a minister.

Robert was the quiet brother, and very little is known about him. Another brother, Mathias, died in childhood as the result of a fall.

The household was so busy by the time Tom arrived that nobody remembered to write down the date of his birth. He was baptized at the Independent Meeting House in Sudbury on May 14, 1727, so probably he was born only a few weeks before that time.

John Gainsborough worked hard to make a living for his family. He manufactured fine woolen cloth and also made hats and clothes. He was kind to the men who worked for him.

The town of Sudbury was famous for woolen cloth, and John Gainsborough would have been happy to teach his sons the trade. But Jack was too busy with his inventions, and Humphrey was too busy with his books. Young Tom was busiest of all with his pencils and paper.

Tom had started drawing as soon as he could hold a pencil. He tried to copy everything he saw. Tom even drew with his penknife. He carved a picture of the headmaster on the schoolroom wall when he was supposed to be studying. He was scolded for drawing pictures of leaves and flowers on the pages of his schoolbooks.

When Tom was eleven years old, his family gave him some paints and brushes. He tried to teach himself to use them. He was never satisfied with the way the pictures looked, but he kept trying.

He painted small pictures of the woods and fields, and of the dogs and donkeys and horses for miles around. He even tried to paint portraits

Tom sketched this view of the gentle Suffolk countryside near Sudbury.

of his brothers and sisters, but it was hard to make them sit still long enough for him to finish the portraits.

Tom liked to play games, too. He played the game of Blind Sim, or blindman's buff. He liked to play "all-hid," or hide-and-seek.

"Let's play leapfrog or follow my leader," Tom called one day to the boys in his class at school during recess.

"No, Tom," a friend said. "You are better than any of us at those games. Let's play bonnety, so we will all have a chance."

"Bonnety it is," Tom said, laughing.

The boys placed their caps in a pile on the ground, then joined hands in a circle around the caps. They pushed and kicked at the pile until one cap was knocked outside the circle. Tom's cap was knocked out, so he had to stand still while the other boys pelted him with their caps.

In the spring of 1739, Tom was almost twelve. He felt he was getting too old for such games. He was tired of school, too. One night he had a long talk with his father.

"It is time for me to start my career, Father," Tom said. "I want to study painting."

John Gainsborough looked at the fair-haired, pink-cheeked boy. Tom was tall for his age and handsome, too.

"I could apprentice you to a house painter," the father suggested. At that time boys went to work at an early age. Many of them learned a trade by working as an apprentice for several years.

"I don't want to slap paint against the side of a house," Tom said. "I think I could do that blindfolded. I want to paint pictures."

"I have heard that there are some good European artists working in London," his father said. "But I don't even know their names."

For centuries the men of England had been sailors and soldiers, merchants and writers, builders and explorers. They made fine cloth and built good furniture. But few of them had been artists.

"We'll talk more about it later," the father said. "After all, you are still a boy in need of a little more schooling."

"I will soon be twelve," Tom protested. "A boy is close to becoming a man at that age."

Seeing that Tom was disappointed, John Gainsborough suggested, "Perhaps your uncle can help you. He knows more about the arts than I do." Tom's uncle was not only headmaster of the Sudbury school, but also a curate of the Church of St. Gregory.

Tom agreed that it would be a good idea to ask his uncle's advice. He whistled on his way up the stairs to bed.

"I won't take a holiday tomorrow," Tom said to himself. "I'll go to school early and talk to my uncle about becoming an artist."

3. "I Must Go to London"

During the next year, Tom had many talks with his uncle about the future.

"I wish we could apprentice you to a great artist," Reverend Burroughs said. "You are old enough now. The great Flemish painter, Sir Anthony Van Dyck, was only ten years old when he became an apprentice."

"Maybe I could be an apprentice to Van Dyck," Tom suggested.

His uncle laughed. "Van Dyck died many years ago. But I will tell you about him, and someday you can learn a great deal from studying Van Dyck's pictures."

Burroughs told Tom of Van Dyck's childhood in Belgium. He explained that, as a child, Van Dyck worked for other painters. By the time Van Dyck was eighteen years old, he was such a good painter that he was made a full member of the Antwerp guild of painters. He painted many religious pictures that were hung on the walls of castles and churches.

Burroughs told Tom that Van Dyck came to England in 1632 at the request of the King of England. The king made Van Dyck a knight and paid him a salary. In return, Van Dyck painted many portraits of the royal family.

"Van Dyck painted so many pictures in England that now we think of him as an English painter," Burroughs said. "During his first year here, he painted the King and Queen a dozen times."

"But I want to paint scenes from nature, not portraits of people," Tom protested.

"My boy, people will pay large sums of money for pictures of themselves," Burroughs said. "I doubt if they will buy landscapes, no matter how beautiful they may be."

"Where can I see some of Van Dyck's pictures?" asked Tom.

"Most of them hang in castles and palaces where lords and ladies live," Burroughs said. "I suppose a few of them might be for sale in the art stores in London."

"Then I must go to London," Tom said. "I must learn from these great pictures how to improve my own painting."

Tom's uncle wrote to a silversmith in London, and the silversmith agreed to help Tom meet some of the London artists. Tom was nearly fourteen before his parents agreed to let him go.

It was Tom's father who made the final decision after Tom showed him some new sketches of the woods near Sudbury. John Gainsborough saw how improved they were over Tom's sketches of a year before. He was amazed at how Tom's skill had developed.

"We won't hold you back any longer," John Gainsborough said. "I will give you the coach fare to London and a few coins for your room and board with the silversmith. Maybe you will change your mind about painting. You might become one of our fine English silversmiths instead."

Tom bounded up the stairway to pack his few belongings. He folded carefully the suits made from his father's woolen cloth. He put in the white shirts his mother had made for him and a scarf knitted by his sister Sarah.

Last of all, he collected his pencils and brushes and paints. He filled the rest of the small packing case with drawing paper.

Tom looked around the room. Should he take his marbles? He had won many a game of plum pudding with those marbles. Or his favorite top? That top had made him the winner of peg-in-the-ring games with the other boys.

"No, I will have no use for tops or marbles in London," Tom said to himself. "I am a man now, and my business is painting."

At the last moment, he reached for one more object. It was a whistle carved for him by his brother, Scheming Jack. Tom had taught himself to play many a merry tune on the whistle.

"No man is ever too old for music," Tom said. "Even a painter likes to make music once in a while."

Tom's mother had tears in her eyes as she embraced her youngest son.

"Don't forget to write, Tom," she said.

"And don't forget that you are always welcome to return home," said John Gainsborough.

Tom's sisters and brothers clustered around to wish him a safe journey. They walked with him down the street to the stop where the big black stagecoach was waiting. Tom climbed inside the coach. He waved to his parents and blew them a kiss. At last he was on his way!

4. The Engraver's Assistant

It was early morning in the year 1740 when Tom Gainsborough arrived in London. As he climbed down from the coach, his eyes blinked with astonishment.

Black smoke from the chimneys clouded the air. The streets of the great city were cluttered with garbage. Brick buildings towered above the noisy streets.

For a moment Tom felt lonely and frightened. Then he felt a friendly hand on his shoulder. It was the hand of the silversmith who had come to meet him.

"London takes you by surprise, doesn't it?" the silversmith said. "There are nearly 700,000 people in this city. And you came here from Sudbury, where there are only a few hundred people."

Tom liked the silversmith at once.

"Do you suppose I can ever find my way around the city?" Tom asked.

"Of course, in no time at all," the silversmith replied. "Come along now, and I'll show you the way to my house."

Tom liked his room at the silversmith's house, and he soon felt at home there. That very week the silversmith introduced the boy to Hubert Gravelot, a French engraver, whose business was making prints of pictures.

Tom showed Gravelot some of the drawings he had made during his schoolboy years in Sudbury.

"Why, these drawings are excellent!" exclaimed the older man. "A bit clumsy, perhaps, but the lines are good. Would you like to work with me and learn the art of engraving?"

An eighteenth century engraver's shop

"As your apprentice?" asked Tom.

"No," Gravelot said. "I think you know enough about drawing to work as my assistant. I will pay you for your work."

Gravelot was old enough to be Tom's father. Tom liked him very much and worked hard to learn the art of engraving. Gravelot taught him how to copy a picture or draw an original one by scratching lines on a metal plate with a graver's tool.

"The graver's tool bites into the metal plate as a farmer's plough cuts into the earth," Gravelot said. "When we have finished preparing the metal plate, many prints can be made from it. Is that not better than paintings which must be done one at a time?"

Tom knew that Gravelot was teasing him. "Nothing is better than painting!" Tom declared.

Yet Tom realized that engraving was a useful skill for a painter. A fine painting could be destroyed by fire or torn by careless handling. An engraving made it possible to make many copies of the painting, so that the picture would not be lost forever.

Also, the careful draftsmanship that went into an engraving was helpful to an artist. It taught him a great deal about drawing. As the weeks went by, the lines in Tom's sketches became more clear and delicate.

As they worked, the Frenchman told Tom about the artists in other countries. He said there had always been artists in Europe.

"Now some of the artists from those countries are coming to England," he said. "I came here because there is great wealth in England. When people have plenty of money, they can afford to buy engravings and paintings for their homes."

One day Gravelot brought out from a cupboard a few dressed-up dolls.

"I thought dolls were only for little girls," Tom said in surprise. "I did not think artists played with dolls."

"Artists work with dolls," Gravelot said. "In the drawings you brought from Sudbury, I noticed only a few pictures of people. Why is that?"

"I used to try to get my brothers and sisters to sit for a likeness, but they moved around after a few minutes," Tom replied.

"Exactly," said Gravelot. "So I shall teach you to make portraits by using the dolls as models. Dolls will sit still forever just as you place them."

As they worked, Gravelot showed Tom how to copy the curving lines of a doll's head and how to sketch in the lines of the arms and hands.

After a few months, Gravelot took Tom to the Academy of Arts in St. Martin's Lane. Gravelot sometimes taught drawing there, and he thought Tom might want to see art students at work.

Tom watched the students in the drawing class. They were trying to sketch the model who stood at the front of the room. Tom did not think their drawings were very good.

In another room students were trying to learn to paint portraits. As they daubed away at their colors, a painting master moved among them to give a few words of advice. The painting master, who appeared to be about 30, was a handsome, well-dressed fellow.

"Most of the teachers here are no better than their students," Gravelot whispered. "This one is different. He is Francis Hayman, a fine painter and a good friend of mine."

Hayman saw Gravelot and Tom standing at the back of the room.

"Good afternoon, Gravelot," Hayman shouted. "And you, young Gainsborough, I have heard of your work. Are you coming to our school to study?"

"No, thank you, sir," Tom said politely.

Tom thought it would be disrespectful to say more. He did not want to tell Hayman that the

students in the class did not seem to be learning very much.

"Do you think you know everything about art?" Hayman asked angrily.

"No, sir," Tom answered. "I sketch well enough, but I know very little about the use of colors. I want to learn more. But not in a school..."

"I know what you mean," Hayman said more calmly. "Artists learn from each other and from experience. Art schools, such as this one, are new in England and not too successful yet. Perhaps you would learn little here."

"You're not angry with me?" Tom asked.

"Because you are too independent to go to school here? Certainly not!" Hayman laughed, shaking his head. "In fact, I would like to invite you and my friend Gravelot to have dinner with me."

Hayman, Gravelot, and Tom walked several blocks to a nearby tavern. They sat down at a table near the fireplace and were soon feasting on mutton pie. Tom enjoyed the conversation. It was the first time he had heard two artists discuss their own work and the work of other painters in London.

"I like you, young Gainsborough," Hayman said after dinner. "I know you have done good work for Gravelot. Would you like to work for me, too?"

Tom was so pleased he could hardly speak. He felt as if he were part of a wonderful dream.

"What kind of work could I do for you?" Tom managed to ask. "I have been drawing since I was a little boy, so I have been of some use to Mr. Gravelot. With painting it is different. I hardly know how to mix the colors."

"I will teach you," Hayman said. "Soon you will be able to paint the background scenes for my portraits. I will paint only the face in a portrait, and you can finish the picture."

Tom felt that he must be the happiest young fellow in the world. Not quite fifteen years old, he was well on his way to becoming an artist.

"We must get Tom home to his room at the silversmith's house," Gravelot said. "If we say any more, he is likely to burst with happiness."

5. Learning to Paint

During the months that followed, Tom was busy all the time. In the mornings he worked for Gravelot, trying to copy the delicate lines of Gravelot's drawings with the graver's tool.

In the afternoons he went to Hayman's painting room, or studio. Tom soon discovered that Hayman paid little attention to drawing. He prepared only rough drawings of the faces he intended to paint, never taking time to pencil in the fine, careful lines that made one face look different from another.

Indeed, Hayman had never bothered to learn to draw well. He was interested more in the use of color to create a beautiful painting. He liked to watch the colors from his brush change a bare canvas into a work of art.

"Now we will prime the canvas," Hayman said one day.

Hayman took the bare canvas on which a portrait would be painted and covered it with a coat of white lead paint.

"Why do you prime the canvas?" asked Tom.

"Priming seals the surface of the canvas," Hayman replied. "If you paint a picture directly on canvas without priming it first, the colors will be absorbed. Some of the colors might run together, and the canvas would be ruined."

As the weeks went by, Tom learned to grind the pigment colors in enough oil to make a sticky mixture. Hayman liked a fairly thick mixture. Tom began to experiment. He tried thinning the mixture with turpentine. Tom preferred a lighter mixture for the pictures he tried to paint on his own.

At first Tom had tried to copy Hayman's brush-work. Before long he could imitate the long, even strokes of Hayman's brush as easily as he had imitated his father's handwriting on the forged excuses from school.

Tom realized he must find his own way to paint. He began to shorten his brush strokes.

One day, after Tom had been with Hayman a year, a rich merchant came to have his portrait made. Tom watched carefully as Hayman started his rough sketch of the man's face before painting the likeness.

"Van Dyck painted a portrait of my great-grandfather," the merchant said proudly. "My portrait will hang beside it in my home." Then he added, "Do you see the clothes I am wearing? This is the same suit my great-grandfather wore when Van Dyck painted his portrait."

Tom could feel his heart pounding with excite-ment. At last he might have a chance to see a picture by Van Dyck!

Hayman soon completed the likeness of the merchant's face in soft colors. He started to paint the clothes the merchant was wearing, an old-fashioned suit with a heavy silk coat and tight breeches. Then he put down his brush.

"Enough for today," he told the merchant.

After the merchant had left the studio, Tom asked, "Why are you willing to paint the merchant in such old-fashioned clothes?"

"Clothes go out of style every few years," Hayman explained. "If we paint a person wearing the clothes of long ago, the picture can never go out of style."

Tom did not think much of that idea. "What a person wears every day is part of the way he looks," Tom said.

"Gainsborough, you have much to learn," Hayman said. "Paint scenes from history. Paint backgrounds from Italy and ancient Greece as the old masters did. Paint costumes, not modern clothes. Paint portraits that flatter the people who sit for you."

"If those are the rules of painting, I don't like them," Tom answered.

Tom wanted to paint landscapes of the English

countryside, not scenes from foreign countries like Italy and Greece. He had never even been to those countries.

If he had to paint portraits to earn a living, he wanted to paint a true likeness. He wanted to paint interesting faces, not the empty blank faces of stupid people.

"I want to make faces look real," he said. "I want to paint people with whatever lines or wrinkles they may have."

Hayman laughed. "Men and women want to look handsome in their portraits," he said.

Hayman cleaned his paint brushes and put them away. He told Tom to finish the portrait of the merchant, painting in the background and the merchant's clothes.

"Shall I paint in your way or my own?" Tom asked.

"Try your own way," Hayman answered carelessly. "The merchant will never know the difference."

For the next few days, Tom worked hard to finish the portrait. This time he did not copy

Hayman's smooth strokes with the brush. He painted the way he liked to paint, using short, choppy strokes. He even tied a stick onto the end of the brush handle so that he could paint while standing further away from the canvas. In this way, he could see what the picture would look like from a distance.

When he had finished, he propped the picture against the wall of the painting room so that a soft light from the window was cast on the picture.

"What do you think of it?" he asked.

Hayman stared in surprise. He had been busy painting and had not watched Tom at work.

"Wonderful, wonderful," Hayman exclaimed. "The silk of the merchant's costume shimmers in the light! Even the jewels in the buckles sparkle as if they were real!"

Then Hayman moved close to the canvas.

"But these brushmarks of yours are so odd," Hayman protested. "These are not the smooth strokes I taught you. They look like the scratches a hen might make in the barnyard."

"Pictures are meant to be viewed from a

distance," Tom said. "And from a distance, this portrait looks as it should."

Hayman agreed. As a special treat, he allowed Tom to carry the portrait across the city to the home of the rich merchant.

The merchant invited Tom to come inside while he studied the portrait. Tom wandered around the big hall. On one wall he saw a portrait in which the colors were rich and deep. The face seemed so real and so sad that Tom wanted to weep.

"You have good taste, young fellow," the merchant said. "That picture is the one Van Dyck painted of my great-grandfather."

Tom studied the portrait by Van Dyck. It was the first great picture Tom had ever seen.

"Hayman made my face more handsome than Van Dyck made my great-grandfather's," the merchant said happily.

Of course, Tom thought to himself. Hayman had not painted the big wart that grew like a strawberry at the end of the merchant's nose.

Tom found other treasures. He saw some small

landscapes, pleasant country scenes like those he had painted in the woods near Sudbury.

"I would like to paint landscapes like these," Tom said.

The merchant laughed. "Nobody would buy them," he said. "These are some little Dutch landscapes given me as a present. People these days want to buy only portraits."

One landscape by Johannes Wynants showed a dusty road winding through the trees with low hills in the background. Another by Jacob van Ruisdael was a meadow scene. The colors were soft, and the pictures looked as if they might have been painted in a dream.

"I must remember the names of these painters," Tom said. "I want to study their paintings."

"You are welcome to return to see my pictures whenever you like," the merchant said.

Tom thanked the merchant, refusing the gold coin offered him for bringing the portrait.

"To see your pictures is reward enough for me," Tom said. "If I may, I will return many times. These pictures can teach me a great deal."

6. "Give Tom a Holiday"

By the time he was seventeen years old, Tom felt like a rich man.

The money he earned from Gravelot paid for room and board. The money from Hayman was spent for paints and brushes, a new set of clothes, and a violin. Tom spent many hours scraping away at the violin as he taught himself to play.

"I wish I could learn enough about music to play with other musicians," he said to Hayman one day.

"Keep at it, Tom," Hayman said. "You have a good ear for music. You are teaching yourself to play the violin, just as you taught yourself to handle a painter's brush."

"You taught me most of what I know about painting," Tom protested.

"Nonsense," Hayman laughed. "I taught you what I know, but you have gone ahead to find new ways of your own. Those strange crisscross brushmarks, for example. Those marks are entirely your own. Someday those brushmarks will make you famous!"

Encouraged by Hayman, Tom began to paint more pictures alone in his spare time. He studied his sketches of the Sudbury countryside. From the sketches he began to paint small landscapes in the soft colors of the Dutch paintings he admired. He placed his landscapes for sale in art shops, but only a few people bought them.

Several men and women asked Tom to paint their portraits. He painted an honest likeness, and they seemed pleased, even though Tom had not flattered them.

Tom found still another way to earn money. He bought some clay and plaster and made small statues of animals — horses, cows, donkeys, dogs, and pigs. Many people liked to buy these little animals as ornaments.

One day Tom had a few spare coins jingling in his pocket. He was careless about money. He always said coins would burn a hole in his pocket if he did not spend them.

With one penny Tom bought a warm bun, munching it as he walked along the street. He gave two pennies to a beggar and two more pennies to a ragged child who looked hungry.

"I still have enough money left to buy a big cup of hot chocolate," Tom said to himself.

As he entered the chocolate shop, Tom noticed an artist's sketchpad on a table. The owner of the pad was a rather plain-looking young man a few years older than Tom.

"May I join you at the table?" Tom asked. "My name is Tom Gainsborough, and I am a painter."

"My name is Joshua Reynolds," said the other. "I am studying to be a painter. I feel that I must study for several more years before I can call myself a painter."

Joshua Reynolds became both friend and rival.

Reynolds, the son of a schoolmaster in Devon, was apprenticed to Thomas Hudson, the portrait painter.

"I want to read all the great books of history and literature so that I can paint a picture with a message like a book or a sermon," Reynolds said earnestly.

"I don't care about reading another book as long as I live," Tom grinned. "I would like to paint landscapes for the rest of my life. Landscapes to me are like music, not like books. It seems to me that art and music go together."

Reynolds said he intended to leave England soon to study in Italy. There he could copy the pictures painted by the old masters.

"But they lived hundreds of years ago," protested Tom. "I want to paint England and the people of England as they are today."

Hayman came into the shop as the young artists were finishing their chocolate. Reynolds greeted Hayman, then excused himself politely and went on his way.

"I have seen some of Reynolds' paintings, and I like them," Hayman said. "You know, Gainsborough, either you or Reynolds may become known someday as the greatest painter in England. I wonder which one it will be."

"Maybe both of us will be great painters," Tom said. "But I don't believe we could ever be good friends. He talks too much of book learning. Perhaps he takes after his father, the schoolmaster."

As Tom and Hayman left the chocolate shop, a heavy fog clouded the air. The fog was so thick they could see only a few feet in front of them.

"In Sudbury the air is probably clear and fresh," Tom said. "Sometimes I wish I could go back there, at least for several months."

"Both Gravelot and I think that you need a rest," Hayman said.

"I wish I were a little boy again," Tom sighed. "I would write myself an excuse, saying 'Give Tom a Holiday.' Then I would go home."

"This time you have earned your holiday," Hayman said.

During the next few weeks, Tom planned a trip home. He bought presents for his parents. He bought a fine new suit of clothes in the latest style. Near the time of his eighteenth birthday, he bought a ticket for the coach to Sudbury.

Tom asked for a ticket as an "outside" passenger so he could ride with the guard and the driver in the open air on top of the coach.

The journey home was merry. Tom made music for the passengers by sawing away on his violin. Sometimes he missed a note when the coach swung round a curve. Once he nearly toppled off, violin and all.

"Keep playing, young fellow," the guard said. "I'll hold tight to your jacket so you won't fall."

There was a happy reunion in the Gainsborough home after Tom arrived in Sudbury. Tom had not written that he was coming, for he wanted to surprise his parents.

His mother could hardly believe that the tall, handsome young man was her son. She gasped as he swooped her off her feet and kissed her.

"Our Tom's come home," she finally called out, wiping the tears of joy from her eyes.

"Welcome home, Tom," John Gainsborough shouted, hurrying to the door to embrace him.

That night Tom told his parents about the city of London. He spoke of his work with Gravelot and Hayman. Then he showed his parents a few of his paintings. They were amazed at the beauty of his work.

Tom reached for his violin to play a few tunes.

"Tom, you always could make music," his mother said happily. "Even on that little whistle your brother carved for you years ago, somehow the tunes came out sweet and clear."

7. Home in Sudbury

Tom Gainsborough was glad to be home. He called on his childhood friends who asked many questions about the big city. He even took time to visit the Sudbury Grammar School from which he had played truant so many times.

After a few weeks, Tom began to spend his days in the woods. Instead of the pad and pencils he had carried to the woods as a boy, he took his brushes, paints, and canvas.

He told a friend, "There is not a picturesque clump of trees, nor even a single tree of any beauty, no, nor hedgerow, stem, nor post that is not pictured in my mind."

One day he was painting the scene before him — a group of trees, with sheep browsing in the meadow below. He was working so hard that he did not realize he had a visitor. A beautiful young lady stood behind him, watching the quick strokes of his brush.

Tom scrambled to his feet, knocking over the small stool on which he had been seated. He felt so awkward that he almost knocked over his tray of paints.

"I'm Tom Gainsborough," he finally said.

"Yes, I know," she answered with a smile. "Everybody in Sudbury knows the famous young painter, Thomas Gainsborough."

"I'm not famous yet," Tom said. "Maybe I might become famous if you would allow me to paint your portrait."

"Would you really like to paint my portrait?" she asked.

"Oh, yes," Tom answered.

She was Miss Margaret Burr, the sister of a young Scotsman who worked for Tom's father. She had come to visit her brother.

Tom and Margaret fell in love. For Tom it was love at first sight. Margaret knew that she was charmed by the handsome young painter. She wondered why he took so long to paint her portrait.

"I'm afraid you will return to your home when I finish the portrait," Tom admitted.

"But you told me you do not like to paint portraits," she teased.

"Only yours," Tom answered. "I would like to spend my life painting portraits of you."

She blushed.

"I love you," Tom said earnestly. "I would like to ask you to marry me, but I do not yet earn enough money to support a wife."

Margaret told him that she had money of her own—not a fortune, but a comfortable income.

"I never knew my father," Margaret said. "He deserted my mother. I do not even know his name, but I have been told that he was a prince or a duke. Each year, through a bank in London, he sends me 200 pounds."

Two hundred pounds in the English money

The young couple chatting in Gainsborough's "Conversation in a Park" are thought to be Tom and Margaret.

of that time would be worth several thousand dollars today. The young couple could live on this sum of money, although there would be little left for luxuries.

"I will work hard at my painting," Tom promised. "Perhaps we will not need to use your money after the first year or two. I shall be earning more money then. Will you marry me, Margaret?"

"I love you, Tom," Margaret said shyly. "I will be proud to be your wife."

Margaret was eighteen years old and Tom was nineteen at the time they decided to marry. Tom wrote to his friends in London asking them to search for a few rooms in which he and Margaret could live.

Margaret told Tom that she did not want a big wedding.

"Big weddings are extravagant and expensive," she said. "We can't afford that."

"Then I shall kidnap you and carry you to London," Tom said.

"No need to kidnap me," Margaret laughed. "I

will follow you willingly anywhere in the world."

Tom's parents were pleased when they heard the news. Margaret was good and kind, and she would make Tom a loving wife.

The young couple left by coach for London, where they were married in Dr. Keith's Mayfair Chapel July 15, 1746.

After the wedding, Tom said, "Let's hire a carriage and go to some fine restaurant to celebrate."

"Oh, no," Margaret answered. "That would be extravagant. Two hundred pounds a year will not allow us such luxury."

Tom sighed, but he had to admit Margaret was right.

8. Tom and Margaret

Tom and Margaret were happy in the rooms they rented in a house near Hatton Garden in London. Margaret kept the rooms tidy, even the room where Tom painted. Sometimes Gravelot, Hayman, and other artists came to see them.

"Come out to dine with us," Hayman said to Tom one day.

"No, I love my own fireside best," Tom replied.

In the evening Margaret would light the candles. Tom liked to paint small landscapes and even portraits by their flickering light.

"Tom, you will strain your eyes in this light," Margaret protested.

"Oh, no, my dear," Tom replied. "Painting by candlelight will give my pictures the beauty of soft lighting."

Tom's terrier, Fox, lay stretched out on the floor beside his master. Margaret held her spaniel, Tristram, on her lap.

Even though Tom and Margaret were happily married, they quarreled once in a while. Margaret thought Tom wasted money. He thought she was too careful with the purse strings. Margaret wanted to meet fine lords and ladies. Tom was happy with musicians, actors, and artists for his friends.

After each quarrel Tom would write a note to his wife. He would sign the note with the name of his dog, Fox, and would address the note to his wife's dog, Tristram. Fox would carry the note to Mrs. Gainsborough.

After the note was delivered to her, Margaret would pretend to take a long time reading it. Then she would write a reply, addressing her note to Tom's dog.

"My own dear Fox," she wrote. "You are

"Tristram and Fox"

always loving and good, and I am a naughty little female ever to worry you as I too often do, so we will kiss and say no more about it." Then she would sign Tristram's name to the note.

Tom knew he was forgiven when Tristram brought the note to him.

One day after they had been married several months, Tom came home with gifts.

"Surprise, surprise!" he called.

"Whatever holiday is this?" Margaret asked.

"We must celebrate," Tom cried excitedly. "I have been invited to paint a picture that will hang on the walls of the new Foundling Hospital."

Tom had brought Margaret a tiny red velvet muff, a lace shawl, and a fan.

"Can you guess what I bought for myself?" Tom waved what looked like a long stick in a leather case.

"Long-handled paintbrushes," Margaret said. "You always like brushes with long handles."

"Guess again," Tom laughed. She wrinkled her pretty forehead but could not think of anything else shaped like a stick.

"It's a flute!" Tom said. He lifted the instrument from the case. "Now I must learn to play it."

Tom taught himself to play the flute very quickly. He still liked to play the violin, too. It was relaxing to make music after long hours in the painting room.

Tom worked especially hard on the picture for the Foundling Hospital. It was a great honor to be one of the artists invited to paint different scenes of London for display on the hospital walls. Tom chose to paint The Charterhouse, which was a school and a hospital.

Tom's painting of The Charterhouse shows sunlight falling on the old building's red-brown stone walls. There are trees in the courtyard on one side. The sky in the background is almost hidden by soft gray and white clouds. Tom gave the picture to the Foundling Hospital in 1748.

"I am sure many people will see and admire the painting," Margaret said. "Some of them surely will want you to paint pictures for them."

The year 1748 was both happy and sad for the Gainsboroughs. Tom and Margaret were

CHARTER
HOUSE.
Gainsborough. 1746.

"Charterhouse"

delighted when their first daughter was born. They named her Mary, but Tom always called her Molly.

Later that year, Tom's father became ill. Tom and Margaret returned to Sudbury so that Tom could be with his father. John Gainsborough died in the autumn.

Tom and Margaret remained in Sudbury for several months to comfort Tom's mother. Tom painted one picture in memory of his father. It was a gentle landscape of Cornard Wood, showing reeds growing by a pond with tall trees nearby. The colors are the golden browns and the gray greens of the English countryside. Gray clouds hang in the sky, yet somehow there is soft light in the picture.

"Tom, I have seen this picture before," Margaret said.

"You have seen the sketches from which this landscape was painted," Tom said. "You have seen my boyish drawings in pencil. I have carried this picture around in my heart for many years. When my father saw my pencil sketches of

"Gainsborough with His Wife and Daughter"

Cornard Wood years ago, he decided to send me to London to study."

"What will you call the picture?" Margaret asked.

* "Oh — 'Woodscene,' or 'Cornard Wood,' or something like that," Tom answered.

Tom was always careless about giving names to his pictures. Nor did he put down the dates when they were painted. He rarely signed his name at the bottom of a picture as other painters did.

"Nobody but Tom Gainsborough would want to paint these scenes of the English countryside," he said, when Margaret urged him to sign his pictures.

Tom would have liked to spend the rest of his life painting landscapes of the woods and meadows, but he knew he must move to a town where there would be portraits to paint.

"I guess my painting will have to be in the 'face way' if I am to earn a living," Tom told Margaret. He meant he would have to paint portraits.

* *In color on page 74*

"We will have to leave Sudbury," Tom continued. "Nobody here is rich enough to buy portraits."

Margaret agreed. "Perhaps we should move to the town of Ipswich," she suggested. "It is not far away. Nearly 10,000 people live there, and it is a busy town."

"A good idea," Tom agreed. "And I could always come back to the countryside from time to time to paint landscapes."

9. Portrait Painter

Tom and Margaret, little Molly, and the two dogs left for Ipswich. They rented a small house with a yard where Molly could play.

Soon after the Gainsboroughs moved to Ipswich, Tom wrote a letter to a friend, thanking him for sending "a few heads." The friend had sent several people to sit for their portraits. Pleased with the portraits Tom painted, they sent others to the studio.

Tom painted their portraits, but he thought many of the sitters were tiresome and stupid.

Tom painted his daughters, "Mary and Margaret Gainsborough," chasing a butterfly on a summer day.

The woods Tom Gainsborough painted as a boy in Suffolk became famous in his glowing painting of "Cornard Wood," or "Gainsborough's Forest."

When Tom tired of fine ladies and gentlemen, he
slipped away to the countryside and painted "The
Shepherd Boy."

75

In this detail from "Mr. and Mrs. Andrews," Gainsborough's neighbors look like stiff doll-like figures set
in the Suffolk countryside.

They knew nothing of art or music, and Tom was bored by their idle chatter about business affairs.

Sometimes Tom sneaked out the back door as one of the Ipswich merchants came in the front door.

"Mr. Gainsborough will not be here today," his wife would say. "Please come back tomorrow for a sitting."

Margaret knew Tom was off to the country for the day. Tom played truant from his own painting room just as he had played truant long ago from the Sudbury Grammar School.

On his trips to the country, Tom painted many small landscapes. He gave some of these pictures to his friends. Sometimes wealthy men asked him to make a larger painting of a landscape, because it was stylish now to hang a landscape above the fireplace. Tom was glad to sell as many paintings as he could, but once in a while he painted only for fun.

One day Tom was walking in a friend's garden where a big pear tree grew. Tom saw a man's

"Tom Peartree"

face peering over the wall. The man was staring at the ripe fruit on the pear tree. His sly, greedy expression showed that he was thinking of stealing a pear.

"Hey, stop there!" Tom shouted.

The man was frightened. He started to run away.

"Stop, man, stop!" Gainsborough called.

"Oh, sir, I meant no harm," the fellow said. "I did not take any of the pears. Please don't report me as a thief."

"Don't be frightened," Tom said, laughing. "I only want to paint your portrait."

"My portrait? What's that?" The poor fellow was more frightened than ever.

"Only your picture," Tom reassured him. "Now wait here. I'll be back in a minute." Tom rushed home to fetch his paints.

"Stand there just as you were, with the light on your face," Tom told the man.

Tom reached for an old board that had been part of a window shutter and began to paint on it. He painted the shabby clothes and the broad-brimmed hat the man was wearing. When Tom started painting the man's face, he noticed that the fellow looked frightened.

"Come now, fellow, look as you did before," Tom told him. "Look at the pear tree, and think how sweet the taste of a ripe pear would be. This garden belongs to a friend of mine. If you manage the right expression, I shall give you two—no, three—of these pears."

At once, the sly, greedy expression reappeared on the man's face. Tom painted swiftly. Here was a face he enjoyed painting because it was full of life, not blank and dull like the faces of some of his sitters. The picture painted on the wooden shutter became famous as "Tom Peartree."

Gainsborough gave the portrait of "Tom Peartree" to a friend who was the editor of the Ipswich newspaper. Philip Thicknesse, Governor of nearby Landguard Fort, saw the picture propped against a wall in the editor's garden. From a distance, he thought Tom Peartree was a real man leaning against the wall.

Thicknesse laughed heartily when he discovered he had been fooled, and that Tom Peartree was only a painting.

"I must meet this painter Tom Gainsborough!" Thicknesse said.

The friendship that resulted was important to Tom. Thicknesse was a rich and influential man. He brought many people to Gainsborough for portraits. Thicknesse was so sure Tom would be famous that he made notes of many of their conversations.

"From these notes I will write your life story someday," he told Tom. And many years later he did.

Gainsborough was not famous yet, however. He charged only a few dollars a portrait. Landscapes he sold for even less money.

But Tom never worried. He was happy with his family. Little Molly was growing up to be a quiet, pretty child, and Tom was very proud of her. A second daughter, Margaret, was born in 1752. She was nicknamed Peggy. Sometimes Tom called Peggy "the Captain" because even as a baby she was the leader of the two children.

Tom was invited to join the Musical Club in Ipswich. This gave him a chance to play his violin and his flute with other musicians. The members met frequently at one home or another for a merry evening of music. There was a great deal of laughter and joking during these evenings, which Tom enjoyed very much.

Tom took Margaret and the little girls for family picnics in the woods. Frequently, he sketched the little girls at play.

By the time Peggy was five years old, she was as tall as Molly. Indeed, the little girls looked almost like twins.

* Tom painted Molly and Peggy chasing a butterfly, playing with a cat, and talking to each other. For some of the pictures, he let them wear the comfortable, loose-fitting clothes of peasant children.

"I like to have Father paint pictures of me," Peggy said one day.

"Mother is sweet and kind to us, too," Molly replied. "When she dresses us to go out, we have the prettiest clothes in Ipswich!"

* *In color on page 73*

"Mary and Margaret Gainsborough"

"Yes, but it is Father who lets us go barefoot," said Peggy. "I like to pull off my shoes and my stockings and wiggle my toes in the grass."

By the year 1759, Tom had painted a portrait of almost every person in Ipswich who could afford to order one. He even made a few trips around the countryside to paint pictures of people in their homes. These portraits were stiff, as if Tom had not always enjoyed painting them. Yet the backgrounds frequently were charming landscapes.

Thicknesse urged the Gainsboroughs to move to the city of Bath in western England. Bath was a fashionable resort visited by many wealthy people. Thicknesse had a home there, as did many rich ladies and gentlemen.

Tom's wife was pleased with the idea of living in Bath. She hoped to meet the ladies and gentlemen of whom she had heard so much. She wanted to make friends with rich people. After all, Molly was now eleven and Peggy was seven. It was time to think about finding them good husbands when they were of marrying age.

10. The Gainsboroughs at Bath

The Gainsboroughs moved to Bath in October, 1759. Tom told his daughters the history of the famous old city. Visitors from other parts of England had come there for centuries to bathe in the healthful mineral springs.

Rich people also visited Bath because it was the fashionable place to be seen. There were fine shops where the ladies could buy ribbons, gloves, and trinkets. Dances were held on the grass in the mornings. At noon there was a concert. Great balls were held on Tuesday and Friday evenings.

Both ladies and gentlemen soon flocked to Gainsborough's studio to have their portraits painted. They thought Tom was shy because he did not listen to their prattle about clothes and parties. Tom thought their talk even more foolish than the talk of the merchants in Ipswich.

In a letter to a friend, Tom wrote, "There is not such a set of enemies to a real artist in the world as they are, if not kept at a proper distance."

He meant that these idle rich people would

The rich and the fashionable promenaded in Bath.

Ison, Walter. The Georgian Buildings of Bath (London: Faber, 1948)

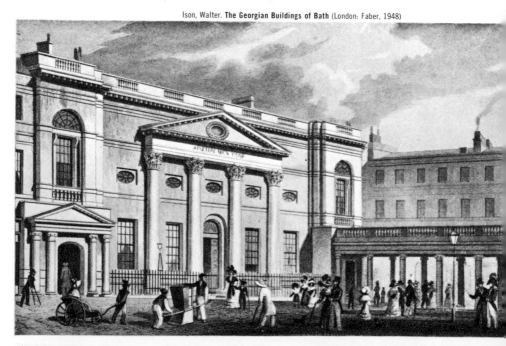

waste so much of his time that no time would be left for painting.

Tom was becoming well known as a portrait painter. He raised his prices. People seemed happy to have a portrait by Tom Gainsborough, no matter what it cost. Sometimes they compared his portraits to those being painted in London by Joshua Reynolds, who was also popular.

Tom still liked to paint country scenes. An elm tree near the road from Bath to London was called Gainsborough's elm because he went there often. Sometimes he took his family with him for a day's outing.

He and Margaret talked about the future of their daughters. Margaret had romantic ideas that the girls would marry men of royal birth.

"Someday they will be fine ladies," Margaret said. "Molly and Peggy will marry rich gentlemen, perhaps even a duke or an earl."

"They may not marry at all," Tom replied. "They may have to earn their living. I think I will teach them to paint draperies and landscape backgrounds for portraits."

So when Molly was twelve years old and Peggy was eight, their father began to teach them to paint. Tom Gainsborough made the painting lessons seem like games.

Peggy was forever asking questions. "What are you painting now?"

"A kit-cat," Tom said.

"But I don't see a kitten or even a cat in the picture."

"Stop teasing me, Peggy," Tom laughed. "You know very well a kit-cat is a three-quarters length portrait. Sometimes people ask me to paint only their heads and shoulders. Sometimes they want a portrait from head to toe. A kit-cat is in between, about three-quarters down."

Molly was able at last to get a word in. "Father, please build a little landscape for us."

"Not until you name the colors of my paints," Tom said.

"There are the reds," said Molly. "Vermilion, light red, Venetian. And the browns: burnt sienna, cologne earth, brown pink."

"Cremona white," interrupted Peggy. It was

the only name she could think of at the moment, so she repeated it. "Cremona white."

"Ultramarine," Molly continued. "Terre verte. And indigo! Yellow-ochre, Naples yellow, yellow lake."

"And Cremona white!" said Peggy.

"Now, will you build a landscape for us, please, Father," Molly begged.

Tom had a special table he used for these scenes, which he called his "thoughts" for pictures. In his earlier years he had painted landscapes as they were. Now he liked to "rearrange" the landscape to make a better composition for a picture.

Gainsborough laid a few pieces of coal on one side of the table to look like rocks. He poured sand from a small bag and made a curving roadway. He placed a few pieces of dried grass against the coal rocks to resemble bushes.

Then he put a small mirror on the other side of the table. The mirror began to look like a lake, as he placed pebbles and bits of grass around the edges.

"Now, go into the kitchen and bring me some broccoli," he said.

Little Peggy ran to the kitchen. She brought back a big handful of broccoli stalks.

"Broccoli stalks make fine trees," Tom said, arranging them like a green forest on the table.

Mrs. Gainsborough came into the painting room. She admired the little landscape scene but asked if she could have the bunch of broccoli to cook for dinner.

"Come, Margaret, I want you to see my new plaything," Tom said, taking her by the hand.

He led her over to a corner of the room to show her what looked like a giant violin.

"What in the world is it, Tom?" Margaret asked.

"A viol da gamba," Tom said proudly. "It is like a bass violin, and the notes are deep and rich."

He plunked away on the strings and then drew the bow awkwardly across the strings. "Oh, I haven't learned to play it yet," he said. "But soon I will learn. And I will make fine music for you during the evenings at home."

"What a child you are, Tom!" Margaret exclaimed. "Yet I love you just as you are. I am sure you and the viol da gamba will spend many happy hours together, and I shall enjoy the music."

11. Fame and Fortune

Tom Gainsborough was making plenty of money now, but he was increasingly bored by many of the people who sat for portraits. He found it hard to be polite to them. He wrote to a friend that he would like to walk away from Bath to "some sweet village" and paint landscapes the rest of his life.

One day an alderman came to Tom's studio, wearing a curled wig and a fancy coat embroidered in gold.

"I wish you to paint my portrait in this fine costume," the alderman said.

Henry E. Huntington Library and Art Gallery
San Marino, California

Gainsborough painted "Jonathan Buttall," the beloved "Blue Boy," in a costume of shimmering blue
satin which reflected the light.

The Duke of Buccleuch and Queensberry, K.T., G.C.V.O.
Drumlanrig Castle, Scotland

The Royal Society of Edinburgh rejected this portrait
of "Henry, Third Duke of Buccleuch" with his dog because it was "too undignified."

A painting of "Mrs. Philip Thicknesse" holding her guitar was livelier than Tom's early portraits. A shocked visitor to his studio said that she appeared both handsome and "bold."

Gainsborough still painted his beloved Suffolk, but the peasants in "The Road from Market" looked a little like the stylish people in Bath.

"The costume does not become you," Tom replied. "I would prefer to paint you in the clothes you usually wear."

"I wish to look like a French king in my portrait," the alderman said. "By the way, when you paint my face, do not forget to put in the dimple in my chin. It is a very handsome dimple, I am told."

Tom threw down his brushes. "I will paint neither your dimple nor your chin," he said.

Yet when Tom found an interesting face, he begged the owner of that face to let him paint a portrait. He liked to paint musicians and actors. Tom begged the actor, James Quin, to sit for him, saying, "If you let me paint you, I shall live forever!"

He painted five portraits of the famous actor, David Garrick. Tom was puzzled by the way Garrick's expression kept changing. It was almost as if the actor's face were made of rubber. By lifting his eyebrows, narrowing his eyelids, pursing his lips, or thrusting out his chin, Garrick could change his entire appearance. When this

Courtesy of the National Gallery of Ireland

"James Quin"

happened, Tom would have to start the portrait over again.

"Actors have everyone's faces but their own!" Tom exclaimed.

In 1761 Tom sent one of the many portraits he had painted to be shown at the Society of Artists exhibition in London. These exhibitions were very important to artists, for they were the only way the public could see works of art. There were no art museums at the time.

The critics who attended the exhibition praised the elegance of Tom Gainsborough's style. They compared his work to that of Joshua Reynolds.

One day, while on a visit to London, Tom met Joshua Reynolds once more in a coffee shop. Reynolds was seated at a table, reading a book.

"I see that you are still a bookish kind of artist," Tom said, jokingly.

"That is true," Reynolds said. "Books mean as much to me as music means to you."

"Both of us have painted portraits of David Garrick," Tom said. "Yet somehow he looks different in your pictures than in mine."

Reynolds smiled. "I have been told that Mrs. Garrick prefers your paintings of her Davey," he said.

When he returned home, Tom told Margaret about the brief encounter with Reynolds.

"Joshua Reynolds is a good man and a fine painter," Tom said. "Yet I could never be a close friend of his. Somehow I find him dull, and I want to yawn after a few minutes of conversation."

Margaret smiled. "I think it is because you will always be a boy at heart," she said. "Joshua Reynolds sounds like an old man in his way of thinking, even though he is still young."

"Perhaps so," Tom agreed. "He learns his lessons from books, and I learn my lessons from nature."

Tom also learned his lessons from Van Dyck's portraits, many of which were hanging on the walls of the great houses in Bath. When Tom went to these houses to paint portraits, he studied the composition and coloring of the Van Dyck pictures in his spare time.

Tom's best portraits were of older men, whose strong character showed in their faces. He also painted beautiful women, paying careful attention to the reflected light in the silks and satins of their dresses.

He still preferred to paint in soft, dim light. Most of his pictures seem to come alive by candlelight. The jewels twinkle, the satins shimmer, and the person in the portrait seems ready to step out of the picture frame.

As Tom made more money, he found more ways to spend money. He continued to buy new musical instruments. He bought five viol da gambas, believing that each new one had a finer tone than the others.

He saw a theorbo in a painting by Van Dyck. A theorbo is a stringed instrument like a mandolin with a long neck.

"If Van Dyck painted a theorbo, it must be a wonderful instrument," exclaimed Tom. "I must have a theorbo!"

He bought a harpsichord, which is like a piano, and taught himself to play it. Peggy also tried to learn to play the harpsichord, but she did not have her father's talent for music.

Tom Gainsborough bought himself a bassoon, a wind instrument that produces a warm bass tone. He puffed away on the bassoon until it seemed as if his cheeks would burst.

"Put it away, man!" cried a friend. "Put it away before you burst yourself!"

Tom enjoyed the hours with his musical instruments, but music was only a relaxation from his real work as a painter.

In 1766 the Gainsboroughs decided to move to a big house in a neighborhood called The Circus. Thirty large stone houses, adorned with stately columns, were built there.

"But the rent on a house in The Circus is so high, Tom," protested Mrs. Gainsborough.

"Nonsense, my dear," Tom answered, "I am earning the money. Why not spend it?"

"The rent is ten times what we paid for our house in Ipswich," she said.

"And the house is a hundred times more beautiful," Tom replied.

The Gainsboroughs enjoyed their fine new home. Tom was a well-known artist now, and many people came to see his paintings. His work was admired by the critics in London.

In 1768 the Royal Academy of Arts was established in London under the patronage of the King and Queen of England. Tom Gainsborough was chosen as one of the original members. The Royal Academy of Arts was in part a school where established artists could lecture to art students. It was also a kind of art gallery where artists could send their paintings for exhibition.

Tom's rival, Joshua Reynolds, was made president of the academy. Reynolds would make a good president, Tom thought.

"He will enjoy giving long lectures on art," Tom said to Margaret. "I think he enjoys lecturing as much as painting."

"And you, Tom, will you give lectures?" Margaret asked.

"Never in this world!" Tom said.

A few months later Reynolds was knighted by the king. He was called Sir Joshua Reynolds now.

"He may be a knight," Margaret said. "But he will never be as good a painter as you."

"Come now, Margaret," said Tom. "Let him paint his way. I'll paint mine."

"Aren't you even a little bit envious, Tom?" asked Margaret.

"I try not to be envious," Tom said earnestly.

Tom admitted to himself that he was interested only in the academy's exhibitions. He did not want to attend the meetings of the members, nor did he want to lecture to the students.

Tom did have one pupil, but he taught him at home. Young Gainsborough Dupont, the son of Tom's sister, had visited in his uncle's house many times. The visits became longer and longer until, by the time the lad was seven or eight years old, he was a member of the Gainsborough household. Tom was teaching him to paint, and the boy said he hoped to become an artist.

"I like your painting room, Uncle Tom," Dupont said.

"Because I have animals there?" teased Tom.

Dogs frequently romped in the studio. A

donkey nibbled on a pile of hay for hours as Tom made sketches of him. Another time three baby pigs played happily around a little trough as Tom watched them from his drawing board.

"It isn't the animals, Uncle Tom," Dupont said seriously. "I like to watch you at work."

"I wish Molly and Peggy felt that way," sighed Tom. "They no longer seem interested in the painting lessons I would like to give them. I hope you will still want to be an artist when you grow up."

12. "The Blue Boy"

One day an ironmonger brought his teen-age son for Gainsborough to paint. The ironmonger was a rich man, and he wanted a full-length portrait of his son.

The boy was wearing an elegant suit of blue satin, with lace at the collar and wrists. In his hand he carried a hat with a curling feather plume. Big bows trimmed his square-toed shoes.

"Your name, young man?" asked Tom.

"Jonathan Buttall," the lad answered.

"They tell me you do not like to paint your sitters in old-fashioned costumes such as my son is wearing," the ironmonger said.

"Usually not," answered Tom. "But somehow, this suit becomes your son. Besides, blue is my favorite color. Yes, Master Jonathan Buttall shall wear this very suit for his portrait."

Tom's nephew Dupont helped him to mix the colors for the portrait.

"Are you sure that blue is a good color for the main part of a picture?" asked Dupont. He was older now and studying painting seriously.

"The sky is blue," answered Tom. "The sea is blue. Lakes and flowers are blue. Why not a blue picture?"

"Sir Joshua Reynolds is said to have told young artists in London that blue is a cold color," Dupont said, hoping his uncle would not be angry.

"Then we shall show Sir Joshua that blue can be painted as a warm color," Tom said.

"Sir Joshua says the big masses of color in a painting must be warm yellow-reds or yellow-whites, because the old masters used those colors," Dupont said.

"Rules, only rules," said Tom.

Dupont watched in amazement as Tom's long

brush flicked away at the canvas in short strokes as delicate as a butterfly's wing. Young Buttall's likeness appeared on the canvas with a sweet and gentle expression. His dark hair curled downward to his shoulders.

The days stretched into weeks as Tom continued work on the portrait. The blue of Buttall's costume began to shimmer and sparkle. There were tiny shadows of greenish brown and deeper blue where the material fell in folds. When the portrait was finished, it was called "The Blue Boy."

Gainsborough's old friend and teacher, Francis Hayman, admired the portrait.

* " 'The Blue Boy' is as fine as if it had been painted by Van Dyck," Hayman told Tom. Young Gainsborough Dupont agreed.

Tom gave his nephew painting lessons every day. In return, Dupont helped with various chores in the studio. Dupont took his work seriously, and Tom had great faith in his future.

"Your painting shows improvement," Tom told his nephew one day. "That velvet coat you have

* *In color on page 93*

"Gainsborough Dupont"

painted looks almost as real as if it had come from my brush."

Dupont was pleased. He tried hard to imitate his uncle's way of painting.

"If young Jonathan Buttall came here now to have his portrait painted, would you allow me to paint the costume?" asked Dupont.

Tom laughed heartily. "No, nephew, that one had to be mine alone," he said. "Remember, you told me I broke all the rules when I painted 'The Blue Boy.' Yet that painting seems to be everybody's favorite."

13. Landscapes

Tom Gainsborough had always been interested in the lights and shadows of nature. He had spent many hours in the fields watching the changing light of the sun from morning until evening He had even tried to paint the changing sunlight into his landscapes.

Now he became concerned about the "outside" light on his pictures. He observed that a picture might look better hung in one place rather than another. His own pictures were at their best in the soft light in which they had been painted.

In a letter to a patron, Tom wrote, "I shall be glad if you'd place your picture as far from the light as possible; observing to let the light fall from the left."

"Lord Vernon"

Gainsborough's pictures needed to be hung properly to show them off to best advantage. Other painters seemed willing to change their style so their pictures would show up well in exhibitions. Gainsborough refused to do this.

As the years in Bath went by, he still painted landscapes whenever he could. These were mostly landscapes painted from memory, or from "arrangements" of nature he created on the table in his studio. These landscapes resembled the Dutch paintings he had admired as a lad, with thick masses of trees, deep shadows, and lowering clouds.

Frequently Tom painted country people and animals into these landscapes. A young farmer talks to a milkmaid. Country folk ride on a farm wagon. Some of these landscapes were painted in oils. Others were done in watercolors, or crayons covered with heavy clear varnish. Tom tried to make crayon drawings look like oil paintings.

Tom liked to include animals in his portraits. He painted Lord Vernon with his hunting dog.

* He painted the Duke of Buccleuch with his favorite shaggy dog in his arms. A little girl named Isabella Franks sat for her portrait with her arms around a pet lamb.

Although Tom charged high prices for portraits, he sometimes gave his landscapes to friends for nothing. One of these friends was Walter Wiltshire, who had a large business hauling goods from Bath to London and other cities. When Tom had pictures to be delivered to London, Wiltshire would send a wagon for them.

"How much do I owe you for delivering my pictures?" Tom asked.

"Not one penny," replied Mr Wiltshire. "It is an honor to deliver the paintings of Tom Gainsborough."

Tom liked to visit Wiltshire at his home in the country. He painted the meadows and the farm animals. An old gray horse carried him about the farm and stood browsing in the grass as Tom painted.

Wiltshire made Tom a present of the old gray horse. In return, Tom gave him a painting called

* *In color on page 94*

"The Harvest Wagon"

"The Harvest Wagon." This later became one of his most famous landscapes.

Tom Gainsborough was generous to all his friends. He gave many of his drawings to an actress, who did not realize their value and used them as wallpaper. The owner of the theater in

Bath gave Tom free season tickets and, in return, was rewarded with the gift of several pictures.

Another friend, Colonel Hamilton, had tried in vain to buy a picture called "Boy at a Stile." Tom liked the picture and refused to sell it. Then he heard Colonel Hamilton play the violin.

He handed the "Boy at a Stile" to Colonel Hamilton.

"But you refused to part with this painting!" Colonel Hamilton protested. "I have tried many times to buy it from you."

Tom laughed. "What I refused to sell, I now give you," he said.

Although Tom was happy to attend plays and concerts with his friends, he still preferred quiet evenings at home. He would paint by candlelight with his wife beside him.

Once Tom was sick in bed for a few weeks. Margaret took good care of him. When he recovered, he wrote to a friend:

"My dear good wife has sat up every night 'til within a few, and has given me all the comfort that was in her power. I shall never be a quarter good enough for her if I mend a hundred degrees."

Tom worried sometimes about his daughters. Molly and Peggy spent too much time day-dreaming about the world of society. Margaret encouraged them in the dream that some day they might meet royalty.

"Maybe you and the girls would like me to buy a coach of our own," Tom suggested to Margaret one day.

"Oh, Tom, it would cost so much," Margaret protested. Then she smiled. "It would be nice," she admitted. "Molly and Peggy and I could go riding every afternoon. Perhaps we could make friends with some of the ladies and gentlemen whose portraits you have painted."

Tom bought the coach. Margaret and the girls went for drives every afternoon. But nobody paid much attention to them. Perhaps they were too quiet and shy.

One day in the year 1774, Margaret told her husband, "Tom, the girls and I are no longer happy here. We would like to live in London. Maybe there you would have a chance to paint the Royal Family, as Sir Joshua Reynolds has done. Then people would have to recognize Molly and Peggy and me."

Tom smiled. He, too, had been thinking of moving to London, but for a different reason. He had quarreled with the officials of the Royal Academy of Arts the previous year because his pictures had been hung with poor lighting. They had also been hung so high on the walls that it was difficult to see them.

"Maybe if I were in London, I could convince the academy officials to break their rules and hang my pictures properly," he said.

His old friend, Philip Thicknesse, wrote many people in London to tell them about Tom Gainsborough. Many were already acquainted with Gainsborough's work and were eager to meet him. Tom rented a fashionable mansion called Schomberg House in Pall Mall.

"Will you drive to London with us in the carriage?" asked Margaret.

"No," answered Tom. "I shall ride to London on the old gray horse Wiltshire gave me."

14. Robbers and Royalty

The Gainsboroughs were happy in Schomberg House. Margaret and the girls had time to ride in the coach, for there were servants to take care of the house. Many of Tom's friends came for dinner or for an evening of music, and they were always welcome.

Margaret still dreamed of the day when their friends would include the ladies and gentlemen of the court, but this did not happen. People came to Tom's studio for portraits, but left without noticing Margaret.

Tom's best friends still were the actors and

musicians with whom he had such good times. One musician was a shy, peculiar fellow named John Christian Fischer, who played the oboe. Tom noticed that Molly and Peggy seemed to like Fischer more than the other visitors who came to Schomberg House.

"I like Fischer as a friend, but I do not want him for a son-in-law," Tom told his wife.

"I had hoped Molly and Peggy would marry into the aristocracy," Margaret sighed. Then she asked, "What is your objection to young Fischer?"

"He seems to be an odd person somehow," Tom replied. "I don't think he has the sympathetic nature that makes for a happy marriage."

Peggy practiced harder than ever on the harpsichord. She hoped to play well enough so that Fischer would pay attention to her. But it was the older sister, Molly, whom Fischer asked to be his wife. Molly and Fischer were married in St. Anne's Church.

"This marriage will not last long," Tom said sadly to his wife.

He was right. The marriage lasted only a few months, and Molly returned home. Fischer, however, continued to visit Schomberg House to see Tom Gainsborough.

Tom worried about his two daughters. They had been such eager, happy children. Now Molly was a sad young woman who seldom smiled, and Peggy spent her time daydreaming that she was a member of the nobility.

Tom worked harder than ever in his studio to forget his worries about his daughters. In his spare time he sought the company of other artists and musicians. Frequently he went to the theater.

Art critics now called Tom "the finest landscape painter alive" and said he was "close on the heels" of Sir Joshua as the best portrait painter.

Tom and Sir Joshua seldom met, as Tom spent most of his time with other friends. Tom never went to the meetings of the Royal Academy of Art. As a member, he was supposed to lecture to the art students occasionally, but he never did. Sir Joshua lectured frequently at the academy and attended all the meetings.

Tom did not like schoolrooms any better than he had as a boy. However, he had been a good teacher to his nephew, Gainsborough Dupont. Dupont was a young man now, able to work as Tom's assistant. Dupont had learned to copy Tom's style of painting so well that only an expert could look at a picture in Gainsborough's studio and tell whether the uncle or the nephew had painted it.

"Oh, pshaw, I can't find my timepiece," Gainsborough said to his nephew one evening. "I must go out to meet friends for dinner. How shall I ever know when to come home without my watch?"

"Take my watch, sir," Dupont said immediately.

That evening Tom was returning home in a carriage when he was stopped by two horsemen. Both men wore their hats pulled down, and each had a strip of cloth like a mask over mouth and chin.

"Halt!" cried one man, aiming a pistol at Tom.

"Your watch and your money," said the other.

"Wait a moment," protested Tom. "The watch

I am carrying is not my own. It belongs to my nephew."

"All the better," said one of the masked men. "It will be your nephew who is the loser, not you."

"Hurry now," said the man with the pistol. "Give us your watch and money at once or I will shoot."

Tom knew the man meant what he said. He gave the robbers the watch and the gold pieces in his pocket. Then he glanced at the face of one of the robbers, or at least the part of the robber's face he could see.

"You remind me of a fellow I used to know," Tom said. "I never knew his real name, but I always called him Tom Peartree."

"You cannot see my face beneath this mask," the robber said. "I am not your Tom Peartree. You will never be able to tell the police who I am."

"I know that you are not Tom Peartree," Gainsborough replied. "But your eyes have the same sly expression. And the way the moonlight falls on your face — I wish I could paint your portrait."

"Nonsense!" exclaimed the robber. "Get along, now."

Two days later the gold watch was found in the pocket of a man who was thought to be one of the robbers. The police returned it to Tom.

"Here is your watch, and thank you for lending it to me," Tom said to his nephew.

Dupont laughed when his uncle mentioned his wish to paint the robbers.

"I believe you would rather paint any rascal or ragged peasant than the King of England himself," Dupont said.

Tom had to admit that was true. Yet he was happy a few months later when King George III summoned him to the palace. The King wanted Tom Gainsborough to paint his portrait and the portraits of other members of the royal family.

Tom became a constant visitor to the palace. One of the princesses said he was "a great favourite with all of the royal family." Queen Charlotte was particularly interested in his work, and Tom allowed her to try her hand at painting with one of his long-handled brushes.

"Queen Charlotte"

Tom painted portraits of every member of the King's house with the exception of the Duke of York. It may be that he painted the Duke of York's portrait and the portrait somehow was lost, but it is thought that the Duke of York's absence from England from time to time is the reason his portrait was not painted.

One portrait of Queen Charlotte ranks among Tom Gainsborough's best paintings. The Queen was a homely woman, but in the Gainsborough portrait she looks almost beautiful in a magnificent dress with laces, ribbons, and ruffles.

"I must make this good little woman look like the queen she really is," Tom told his nephew. "The dress and the ornaments will help me to do so."

Artists and art critics too marveled at the beauty of Tom's work. One of the critics said, "Gainsborough made even our old Queen Charlotte look picturesque."

15. "Fancy Pictures"

Gainsborough frequently painted small figures of country folk and farm animals into his landscapes. When he was about 50 years old, he began to paint large pictures of them.

These "closeups" were called "fancy pictures," probably because it struck his fancy to paint them. Tom Gainsborough valued these "fancy pictures" so highly that he charged more for them than for his landscapes or portraits.

One of Tom's best pictures of this kind was
* called "Girl with Pigs." It showed a gentle little

* *In color on page 131*

"Mrs. Siddons," the famous actress, sat for her portrait in a gown of striped satin. A critic saw the painting and said, "This is genius."

Beaverbrook Art Gallery
Fredericton, New Brunswick

Because it pleased Tom's fancy to paint ragged country children, paintings like "Peasant Girl Gathering
Faggots" were called "fancy pictures."

Gainsborough used live pigs as models in his studio
in order to make his "Girl with Pigs" more realistic.

Sir Alfred Beit, Bt.
Russborough, Ireland

The sad-eyed "Cottage Girl," holding a pitcher and
bowl, is thought by critics to be the best of Gainsborough's "fancy pictures."

peasant girl in a ragged dress watching little pigs eat from a round bowl. When this picture was exhibited, everybody liked it.

An old farmer who saw the picture said, "They be deadly like pigs, but nobody ever saw pigs feeding together but what one of them had a foot in the trough."

At the same time, an art critic wrote this poem about the picture:

And now, o Muse, with songs so big,
Turn round to Gainsborough's Girl and Pig,
Or Pig and Girl, I rather should have said;
The pig in white, I must allow,
Is really a well painted sow:
I wish to say the same thing of the maid.

Sir Joshua Reynolds admired the picture. He bought it from Tom for a high price:

In thanking Sir Joshua for buying the picture, Tom wrote, "I may truly say I have brought my pigs to a fine market."

Many people were surprised that Sir Joshua,

"Girl with Pigs"

the scholar, liked this simple picture of a barefoot peasant girl watching little pigs. Some even suggested that Sir Joshua bought it to hang beside finer paintings so that Tom Gainsborough's work would look foolish. This was not true. Sir Joshua admired the painting, although he said he wished Tom had made the peasant girl look a little prettier.

Sir Joshua kept the painting in his own collection for years, and told a friend it was the best painting Tom Gainsborough had ever done. When Sir Joshua finally sold "Girl with Pigs" to a friend, it was valued at several times more than he had paid for it.

Tom and Sir Joshua had become somewhat closer as they grew older. Indeed, Tom planned to paint Sir Joshua's portrait. He made several sketches, but for some unknown reason the portrait was never painted.

Tom Gainsborough was happiest when painting his "fancy pictures." A friend said Tom's face always took on a gentle, pleased expression at the sight of peasant children at play.

One day while walking near his home in London, Tom was approached by a beggar woman with her handsome small son. The little boy's name was Jack Hill.

"Here are a few coins for you, poor woman," Tom said. Then he looked at the boy closely.

"I would like to take your little boy home with me," he said.

"What would a fine gentleman like you see in a small beggar boy?" the woman asked.

"I would like to paint his picture," Tom said.

"Would you feed him well?" asked the woman.

"He will have the best of everything," promised Tom.

"Would he have a place to sleep?" she asked.

"He will have a bed of his own with plenty of quilts to keep him warm," Tom said.

The mother left her son in Tom's care at Schomberg House.

Margaret Gainsborough, Molly, and Peggy liked the little boy at once. They scrubbed off the dirt and dressed him in clean clothes.

"Oh, Tom, the girls and I would like to adopt this little fellow," Margaret said.

"He is a handsome boy indeed," said Tom.

Tom painted Jack Hill as a little shepherd boy, but he had a hard time coaxing the boy to stay in his studio even a few hours. After a few days Jack Hill ran away to search for his mother. Tom found him a few blocks from Schomberg House and brought him back. Once more Jack

Hill ran away, and Tom had to find him again.

The beggar woman finally came to see the Gainsboroughs at Schomberg House.

"I need my son with me," she said. "I know you have taken good care of him here, but I miss him."

Jack Hill cried with joy as his mother put her arms around him.

"Promise that you will bring him back to see us from time to time," said Margaret Gainsborough.

The beggar woman promised. Then she walked away, holding her son tightly by the hand.

Tom continued to paint these "fancy pictures" whenever he could escape from work on his portraits of elegant ladies and gentlemen in their fine clothes and jewels.

* He painted a peasant girl gathering sticks for the fire in the cottage where she lived. He
* painted a barefoot child with a milk pitcher in one hand, holding a small fat puppy in her arm. He painted another country girl carrying a bowl of milk. In one picture, called "Child with a Cat — Morning," Tom painted a little boy followed

* *These paintings in color on pages 130 and 132*

"The Wood Gatherers"

closely by his pet cat. The cat looked so close and so real that anybody who looks at the picture wants to reach out a hand to stroke the cat's fur.

As Tom grew older, he depended more and more on his nephew, Gainsborough Dupont. The nephew helped Tom in his studio and also painted portraits of his own, but he never really made a name for himself except as an expert imitator of his uncle.

"I can imitate your portrait style well enough," Dupont said one day. "I can even imitate your landscapes, though not as easily. But I shall never be able to imitate these 'fancy pictures' of yours, no matter how hard I try."

"Keep trying," laughed Tom. "Perhaps the secret is that I paint these pictures of simple people from the heart."

16. The "Eidophusikon"

As Tom grew older, he no longer stayed at home evenings to paint by candlelight. Frequently he went to the theater in Drury Lane, where his friend David Garrick was often the star.

One night after the play was over, Garrick introduced Tom to the theater's stage designer, Philippe Jacques de Loutherbourg.

"I have heard of you, sir," Tom said. "Aren't you the man who knows how to make pictures that move?"

De Loutherbourg laughed. "You might call them moving pictures of a sort," he said. "I try to paint once in a while, but my pictures are not very good. What interests me most is the effect light can have on a painted scene."

"You are a man after my own heart," Tom said excitedly. "I have been interested in light and shadow since I was a boy. But how can you make pictures move by the use of light?"

"Come to the theater tomorrow night, and I will show you," de Loutherbourg promised. "If you arrive here an hour before the play begins, you can see my invention."

Tom arrived early at the theater the following evening. He saw that de Loutherbourg had drawn the curtains on the stage almost closed.

"Sit close to the stage so that you can see my pictures," de Loutherbourg told him.

Then de Loutherbourg placed a transparent panel in the small open space between the stage curtains. Painted on the panel was a ship on a stormy sea.

"Now watch what happens when I light

candles behind the panel," de Loutherbourg called.

Tom was amazed. The flickering light of the candles behind the painting seemed to set the picture in motion. The waves seemed to break in whitecaps as the flames burned high, then to calm down as the flame grew dim. Jagged streaks of lightning seemed to come down from the gray storm clouds.

"How wonderful!" Tom exclaimed. "What do you call this invention of yours?"

"I call it my Eidophusikon," replied the stage designer.

Tom laughed. "I can't even pronounce the word, but I must try my hand at this kind of painting."

Tom always had fun when he tried something new. This seemed to be the most fun of all. He bought many small panes of clear glass. On the glass he painted landscapes and seascapes, now called his "Peepshow Landscapes."

One of these landscapes on glass shows a small cottage nestled beneath the trees. When Tom

Victoria and Albert Museum, London. Crown Copyright

"Peepshow Landscapes"

lighted a candle behind the glass panel, soft light came from the cottage window and door as if the farmer inside the cottage had turned on the lights for the evening.

Other small paintings on glass show sailing vessels in a harbor, quiet meadows, and country scenes. By lighting candles behind the glass panes, Tom tried to imitate the effect of sunlight, moonlight, and even the light of an open fire.

"How do you like my glass pictures?" Tom asked Margaret.

"They are charming," Margaret replied. "My dear Tom, what a child you still are! You have as much fun with the glass and candles as if they were new toys."

"I am nearing old age," Tom laughed, pointing to his gray hair. He knew Margaret was teasing him.

"Life has always been a happy game for you," Margaret said. "Remember how you used to play with the dressed-up dolls —"

"Margaret, you know very well I worked with the dolls," Tom said.

Margaret continued, "Remember how you made little landscapes on the table for Molly and Peggy when they were children?"

Tom laughed. "Perhaps you are right," he said. "Perhaps a painter never really grows up, because he has to see this wonderful world through the clear eyes of a child."

Then Tom turned back to his small pictures on glass.

"Let me show you just one more," he said. "Look at this little painting of mountain scenery. When I light the candle behind it, can't you almost see the soft light of the moon in the picture?"

17. Gift of a Genius

Every year there was an exhibition of paintings at the Royal Academy of Art, and every year Tom Gainsborough quarreled with the officials as to how his pictures should be hung.

One of his best paintings had been placed high on a chimney board above a fireplace where it could hardly be seen. Another painting had been placed in too strong a light so that the delicate colors almost seemed to fade. Several times Tom's pictures were placed too high for proper viewing. One picture was even hung above a door.

In 1784 Tom exhibited his paintings in his home at Schomberg House. He invited his friends, and they in turn invited other people. The exhibition was a success, and Tom decided to have his own showing every year. He no longer needed to exhibit his paintings at the Royal Academy.

Tom worked as hard as ever, but he could tell he was getting old. Somehow he felt he would not live much longer. He did not know why he felt this, except perhaps that he tired easily. One day in 1787, he paid a visit to the home of Richard Sheridan, the well-known playwright. Sheridan was an old friend.

"I think I shall die soon," he told Sheridan. "I have many acquaintances, but few friends. I wish to have one man worthy to accompany me to the grave. Will you come to my funeral?"

Tom was mistaken. He had many true and loyal friends. Yet somehow he felt lonely.

"Of course, I will grant your request," Sheridan said, thinking Tom was imagining some ailment. Tom smiled and said no more.

Unfortunately, Tom was not imagining his sickness. He was seriously ill with cancer, and at that time cancer was one of the many diseases that doctors were unable to cure.

During the days when he felt well enough, he touched up with his brush the picture he was sure would be his masterpiece. The picture had really been finished for months, and there were rumors that the King admired it.

Tom called this picture "Woodman." The idea for the picture had come to him when he saw a poor old man, tired from a lifetime of hard work. Tom took the poor man home and cared for him. In return, the man posed for Tom. The old man was happy to stand in the warm room while Tom painted his picture.

Tom painted him standing under a tree, with a cottage in the background. A violent storm rages about him, and the man's small dog huddles near him. The dog's head is turned as if to watch a bolt of lightning cross the sky.

Tom wrote a letter to Sir Joshua Reynolds about the picture. The letter, which has been

"Self-Portrait—1787"

preserved in the Royal Academy of Arts, reads as follows:

"Dear Sir Joshua,

I am just to write what I fear you will not read — after lying in a dying state for six months. The extreme affection ... which Sir Joshua has expressed induces me to beg a last favor, which is to come under my Roof and look at my things. My Woodman you never saw. If what I ask now is not disagreeable to your feelings ... I can from a sincere Heart say that I always admired and sincerely loved Sir Joshua Reynolds. Signed — Tho. Gainsborough."

Sir Joshua came to see Tom soon after receiving the letter. They talked for several hours of all that had happened since their first meeting as students in the chocolate shop in London. They even talked of the influence the great paintings of Van Dyck had on both of them.

"I followed the old rules of painting and made a few new rules of my own," Sir Joshua said. "You painted in your own way from the start, yet somehow you managed to create paintings of great beauty."

"And I have always said even the worst painting you ever did was far better than anything the rest of us could achieve," Tom said earnestly.

Sir Joshua bade Tom farewell. After he left the room, Tom said in a tired but happy voice, "We are all going to heaven, and Van Dyck is of the company."

Gainsborough made out his will. He left his painting materials and a small sum of money to his nephew, Gainsborough Dupont. He knew Dupont could earn a good living for himself in the future as a painter. The rest of his money, his pictures, and drawings were willed to Margaret. There was also a sum of money in the bank to take care of Margaret and the two daughters.

"I am ashamed to leave you so little, my dear,"

Tom said on his death bed. "You were right all through the years in pleading with me to save more. I was wasteful, and now I repent."

Tears flowed down Tom's cheeks. He reached for Margaret's hand and kissed it.

"There, there, Tom," his wife said. "I have always loved you as you are. I knew you were generous and impulsive when I married you."

"But now you and our daughters will have to pay for my extravagance," Tom said. "You will not be able to live in comfort on what I have to leave you."

"You are mistaken, Tom," Margaret said. "We have far more than you think. During the years of our marriage, you always gave me far more money than I needed. Year after year I set aside some money for a rainy day. The money I saved is now plenty to take care of us."

Tom smiled in relief.

"My dear, sweet Margaret," he said. "Somehow you have always taken good care of me, and I know you will care for our daughters in the same way."

Tom held Margaret's hand in his. "Let's pretend Molly and Peggy are happy little girls again, playing barefoot in the garden," he said. Tom closed his eyes and drifted off to sleep with a smile on his face.

He died in his room at Schomberg House August 2, 1788.

Sheridan was one of the mourners at Tom's funeral, as he had promised to be. So was Sir Joshua Reynolds, who told Margaret he would do all he could to help in the sale of Tom's paintings and in any business matters that might arise. The artists and musicians Tom had loved also were there, as was Jonathan Buttall.

After the funeral one friend said, "Tom Gainsborough once wrote me that we love a genius for what he leaves, and we mourn him for what he takes away."

"Tom Gainsborough's merry wit and music are gone now," said another friend. "But he has indeed left us the gift of a true genius in the hundreds of paintings from his brush."

Index